ALLEN PHOTOGRAPHIC GUIDES

DRI

CONTENTS

BEFORE MOUNTING THE BOX SEAT

USE OF A DRIVING APPARATUS

It is advisable that, prior to taking up the reins on the box seat for the first time, the basic driving skills are practised on a driving apparatus. This does not have to be an elaborate device as shown in the photographs; two leather dog leads attached to small bags of sand hung over the back of a chair will suffice. What you must remember, however, is that a driving apparatus will always give a 'dead' feel in your hand. When you come to drive a horse, or pony, you will find that the feeling you have in your hand, through the reins and the horse's mouth, will be quite different. This feeling is known as **contact**.

WHAT IS CONTACT?

Contact is a form of communication between the driver and the horse, via the reins. It is not dissimilar to a telephone system. If the telephone line is bad and the connection poor then your conversation will be intermittent but if the line is well maintained, every word will be crystal clear. As with a telephone conversation, contact is a two way thing. Through a steady and consistent feel via the reins, your horse will understand your needs and await your directive. As your driving skills improve you will be able to interpret the response the horse gives from his mouth through the reins into your hands.

The bit in the horse's mouth should lie cushioned on his tongue and should not be pulled against the sensitive bars of the mouth. That is why it is vital that relaxed and supple wrists are developed and that a sympathetic and consistent feeling of contact is maintained at all times.

Contact is not the only form of communication that you have with your horse. Your voice and the whip are also vitally important when it comes to control. These three things, your **voice**, the **reins** and the **whip**, are collectively know as **the aids**.

THE AIDS

The three main communicative aids are of equal importance.

The voice The use of the voice is far more important with driving horses than with riding horses. It replaces the sensation of touch as it is not normally possible to pat your horse as a form of praise or for reassurance when driving. The beginner must learn how to alter the tone of their voice so as to be able to praise, reassure, cajole, request, demand and, at times, reprimand. The horse has a very acute sense of hearing, and there is nothing more upsetting to a horse than being shouted at. A quiet and authoritative voice is all that is required, especially in times of stress! For the words of command, such as 'walk on' or 'trot on' a crisp and energetic tone should be used whilst soothing tones should be used for slowing down. Think of *'jolly for go and lullaby for slow!'*

The reins Directional commands are given by applying pressure, via the reins and bit, to either the right or left side of the horse's mouth. The amount of pressure will depend on the sensitivity of the horse's mouth, the degree of turn, the speed you are going and the type of carriage you are driving. How much or how little pressure is required with each individual horse is something that can only be learnt by experience,

and driving many different horses. What is consistent with all horses is that, when turning, they must be *allowed* to make the turn by having the freedom to stretch the outside of their body. When driving a turn, try to remember *'feel and yield'*.

Speed is controlled by your voice and by pressure on both reins simultaneously. Pulling backwards on the horse's mouth every time you wish to slow down, will teach the horse to set his jaw against the pain in his mouth. This will result in loss of control rather than gaining control and, ultimately, if the horse is habitually driven in this manner, he will become what is known as 'a puller' and very uncomfortable to drive. By closing the fingers firmly around the reins with a retaining feeling you will apply pressure across the horse's tongue and indicate he is to slow down. If slightly more pressure is required, close the upper arm and elbow to your side and press your feet against the foot rest. This will brace your back, thereby applying more pressure without pulling backwards on the horse's jaw. With forward transitions, such as halt to walk, soften the arm forward because the horse must be allowed to lower his head and slightly stretch his neck in order to put his shoulders into the collar to start the carriage.

The whip The whip is not an instrument of punishment or torture, it is used to encourage the horse to go forwards and can also be used to assist in aiding a turn. In other words, if the driver's voice replaces the rider's hand, then the driving whip replaces the rider's legs! The stock of the whip should be long enough to ensure that the lash of the whip can be placed between the collar and the saddle without the driver having to lean forward.

It is a golden rule of driving that when seated on the box seat you should always have the whip in your hand, and not in the whip socket. You never know when your horse or pony might take fright and start to run backwards or sideways, possibly resulting in a nasty accident. When using a holly whip it is inadvisable to flick the lash as this could result in the quill being broken or the lash becoming entangled in the harness. Using a supple movement of the right wrist the lash should hit (as opposed to miss) the horse on the shoulder between the collar and saddle. It is not a good idea to use the whip on the horse's hindquarters as this could encourage a buck or a kick. The other golden rule regarding a carriage driving whip is that it is *never* cracked.

WHY DRIVE WITH THE COACHING HAND?

The simple answer to the above question is that it is not necessary to drive with the coaching hand but there are several reasons why most driving enthusiasts consider that

the coaching hand is the safest and most efficient means of driving horses.

The comfort of the horse If the horse is happy in his mouth then he is more likely to be happy in his work. If both reins are held in a secure and even manner in the left hand the horse is less likely to have his mouth indiscriminately jabbed. Directional aids will be consistent in their application and the slowing aids will be given evenly on both reins.

Driver/passenger safety Should it be necessary to shorten both reins quickly, this can be done without fear of dropping a rein. If it is necessary to apply the whip, to avoid an accident, then the right hand is free to do so. Likewise, if it is necessary to give hand signals to other road users, the driver's right arm and hand can do so.

Progression Having acquired the skills to drive a single or pair in the classical coaching manner, you will find that it is a natural progression to place two more reins in your hand and drive a tandem or a team.

HOLDING THE WHIP AND REINS

THE WHIP

The whip is held against the palm of the right hand and the index finger by the bulb of the thumb and the thumb itself. The lower three fingers should be free of the whip to enable them to be placed through or on the reins. The whip should be held at the point of balance which is most usually at the top of the hand piece as this allows the weight of the hand piece to stabilise the whip in the driver's hand.

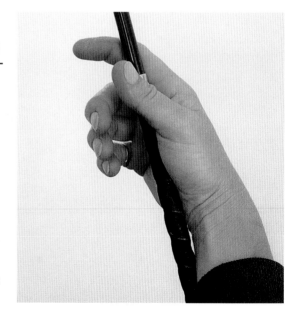

THE REINS

The left rein is placed over the index finger of the left hand, and the right rein is placed between the middle and third finger of the left hand. The left rein should lie on top of the right when held in the palm of the hand.

AUTHOR'S NOTE

If the driver has a very small hand then a more secure hold on the reins can be achieved by placing the right rein between the index and middle finger.

When holding the reins in the left hand, the lower three fingers squeeze the reins into the palm of the hand, while the thumb and index finger are held relaxed.

AUTHOR'S NOTE

Should the thumb and index finger be clamped onto the reins the driver's wrist will become rigid. This will restrict the rotation of the wrist and make the driver's arm and shoulder ache. More importantly it will cause great discomfort in the horse's mouth.

The wrists of both hands should be held relaxed and in a slightly rounded position. The left hand should be held approximately six to eight inches from the front of the body. The right hand, holding the whip, should be held close to the left.

From the box seat Note the position of the whip. This should be held with the tip of the whip at '11 o'clock'. This will keep the lash of the whip off the horse's hindquarters and reduce the risk of hitting your passenger in

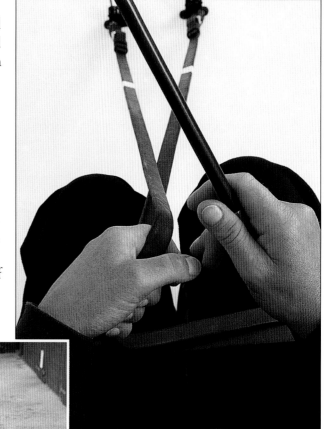

the face! More importantly, by keeping the whip in this position the driver's right hand will be correctly positioned for placing on or through the reins.

AUTHOR'S NOTE

Because the driver is sitting to the right of the horse the left rein has to be slightly longer than the right. This can be clearly seen by the fact that the left rein splice* is slightly in advance of the right. *To acquire the length needed for driving reins, each rein is made up from two lengths of leather. the point at which these lengths are stitched together is known as a rein splice.

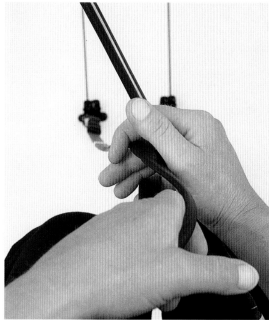

It is often necessary to support the left hand with the right. To do this place the middle and third fingers of the right hand between the reins. It is important that the whip is maintained in the correct position, and by doing so the right hand will always be in the correct position to be placed through the reins. The fingers of the right hand can then be closed around the reins for additional support.

Some people prefer to place the lower three fingers of the right hand between the reins (see above), this is also correct.

AUTHOR'S NOTE

Take care not to press downwards onto the left rein as this could encourage the horse to veer to the left.

TURNING LEFT AND RIGHT (Degrees of turns)

INCLINES

To make a slight incline to the left, rotate the left wrist so that the knuckles are uppermost, the left rein is shortened and the right rein is lengthened, this tells the horse to move a little to the left. (The white tape on the reins indicates the rein splices.)

From the box seat Note the relaxed thumb and rounded wrist and that the driver's elbow is still held close to her side.

AUTHOR'S NOTE

Remember it is the lengthening of the outside rein that allows the horse to turn.

To make a slight incline to the right, rotate the left wrist so that the thumb is turned towards the horse and the finger nails are uppermost, the right rein is shortened and the left rein is lengthened.

From the box seat Note that the lower three fingers are closed around the reins, and that the index finger has been slightly extended to apply a little more pressure to the right rein. The thumb, wrist and elbow are relaxed.

SHARPER TURNS

When a sharper turn has to be negotiated, it might be necessary for the right hand to assist the left.

To pick up a rein with the right hand take hold of the rein from *above* the rein, using the lower three fingers. By pressing the rein against the leather of the hand part of the whip you will have a far better grip of the rein. The right thumb must not be placed under the rein as this will result in loss of control of the whip and the possible danger of the lash becoming entangled in the axle of the carriage.

To turn left with the right hand assisting, take up the left rein as shown above. With a supple movement of the right wrist, indicate to the horse the degree of turn and allow the horse to make the turn by rotating the left wrist as when making an incline to the left.

AUTHOR'S NOTE

Although the movement of the right wrist should be upward and backward, in this photograph the right hand has been raised rather too high to show the hand position clearly.

To turn right with the right hand assisting, take up the lower, or right, rein with the right hand, in the same manner as you would the left rein. Again, using the rotating motion of the right wrist to make the palm of the right hand turn towards you, indicate to the horse your desire to turn right. At the same time allow the horse to make the turn by dropping your left thumb forwards towards the horse's tail.

The same action viewed from the box seat.

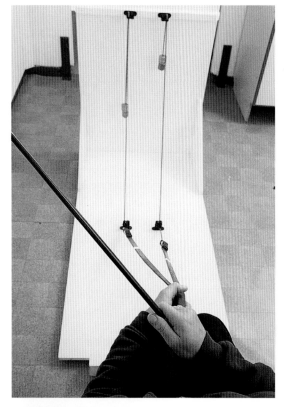

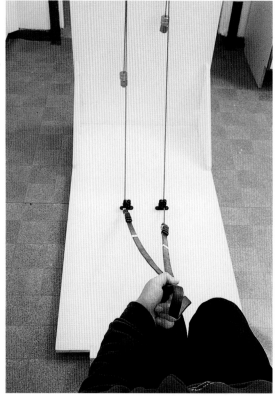

Sometimes when making a sharp turn to the left or right it is necessary to have your right hand free of the rein, maybe to indicate to traffic or to use the whip. On these occasions it would be necessary to 'take a loop'.

To take a loop to the right, pick up the right rein then draw the rein back towards you under your raised left thumb. Secure the right rein by pinching the left thumb down onto the right rein, enabling you to remove your right hand.

AUTHOR'S NOTE

Always bring your right hand back towards your left and never drop your left hand forwards to catch the rein. If you were to do this you would lose contact with the opposite rein and veer off to the left or right.

◄ *Taking a loop viewed from the box seat.*

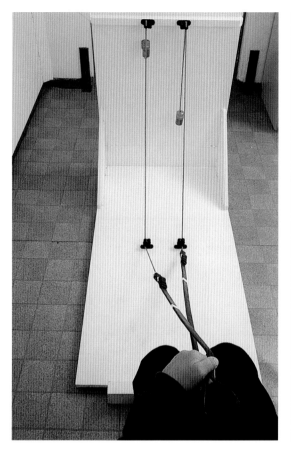

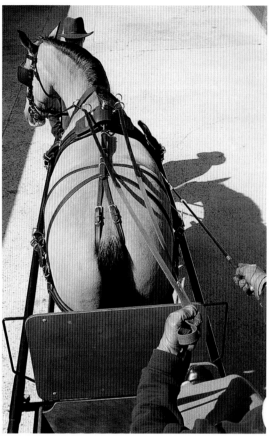

To take a loop to the left, follow the same procedure but bring the left rein back under your left thumb.

From the box seat The photograph above shows how the whip can be used against the horse's ribcage on the opposite side to the direction of the turn to assist in making the turn.

SHORTENING AND LENGTHENING THE REINS

SHORTENING

To shorten the reins, place the right hand through the reins, as shown in the photographs on page 7, approximately six inches in front of the left and close the fingers firmly around the reins. Then soften the fingers of the left hand but do *not* remove the left hand from the reins. Push both reins back through the left hand with the right to shorten them to the required length (*see top photos on page 14*). Close the left hand on the reins and remove the right.

> **AUTHOR'S NOTE**
>
> This method of shortening the reins is not advisable in an emergency as the reins can buckle when being pushed back through the left hand.

To shorten both reins quickly, place the right hand directly behind the left and take hold of both reins between the thumb and index finger *(above)*. Soften the fingers of the left hand but do not remove them from the reins. Simultaneously bring the right hand back towards the body and slide the left hand down the reins, thereby shortening both reins equally and smoothly *(right)*.

AUTHOR'S NOTE

Care should be taken not to hit your passenger in the face with the whip when shortening the reins in this manner.

Should it be necessary to make an instantaneous halt (emergency stop) to avoid an accident, or to bring a wayward horse under control, place the right hand through the reins approximately 12 inches in front of the left, and take a sharp downward pull on the reins. At the same moment pull upwards, firmly, with the left hand.

LENGTHENING

To lengthen the reins, follow the photographs at the top of page 14 but instead of pushing the reins back through your left hand, ease the reins forward out of your left hand to lengthen them. It is also possible to shorten or lengthen one rein only by closing the right hand on the particular rein and softening the left hand on the same rein while, at the same time, not allowing the opposite rein to slip.

AUTHOR'S NOTE

Take care that you do not allow the reins to lengthen by letting them slip through your hand in an uncontrolled manner, or to let the horse 'take' the reins through your hand. Any adjustments to the length of the reins should be made using the right hand.

MOUNTING AND DISMOUNTING THE VEHICLE

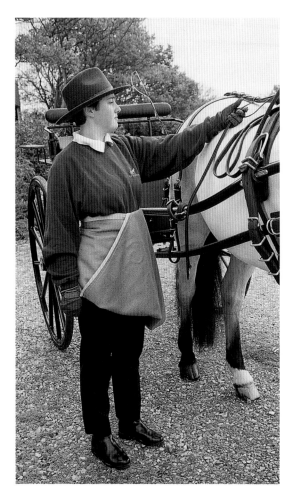

MOUNTING

When preparing to mount the vehicle from the right, take the reins in your left hand, pull them loose from the back strap and step to your left towards the carriage. Place your right hand through the reins, and take up the spare loop of reins under your right thumb. Holding the reins in this manner makes it possible to take hold of the hand rail whilst mounting the vehicle, without loosing control of the reins.

Step quickly and quietly into the vehicle, paying close attention to your horse at all times. Sit down immediately and take the reins in your left hand. Arrange your apron and pick up your whip. You will note that the whip has been lain against the passenger seat and is not in the whip socket. This is because it is possible to break the whip when mounting the carriage. The disadvantage of the whip being placed against the seat is that you have to stretch over your body with the right arm to pick it up.

AUTHOR'S NOTE

Do not hold the whip in your right hand when mounting the carriage from the right. It is possible to hit your horse on the hindquarters when stepping into the carriage, which could result in the horse jumping forwards.

When mounting the vehicle from the left, follow the same procedure for mounting from the right, but take the reins up in the left hand. The disadvantage of this method is that you have to step across the passenger seat and up onto the box seat but the advantage of this method is that the reins are in the left hand throughout the mounting procedure and that the whip is ready by your right hand as soon as you sit down.

AUTHOR'S NOTE

The main advantage of mounting the vehicle from this side is that you are on the kerb side of the carriage and therefore away from the traffic.

DISMOUNTING

Dismounting the vehicle is a reversal of mounting, regardless of from which side of the vehicle you dismount.

AUTHOR'S NOTE

When dismounting the vehicle remember to always face into the carriage and to step out backwards, then should the horse jump forward you will be able to step back into the vehicle and sit down quickly to regain control. If you were to step down facing out of the vehicle you would be far more likely to slip and hurt your back.

POSITION ON THE BOX SEAT

The driver is seated in a comfortable and secure position, with her feet firmly placed on the foot rest and her back resting against the back rest. Her upper arms are held in a vertical position close to her body, and her lower arms are held in a near horizontal position with relaxed and rounded wrists.

SOME COMMON REIN HANDLING FAULTS

Clenched left fist with wrist broken backwards
Not only will the driver's hand, arm and shoulder become very tired, but also the ability to rotate the wrist will be lost. This will also result in considerable discomfort in the horse's mouth.

Clenched fist held flat
Again, this fault will make the driver's hand, arm and shoulder tired, the ability to rotate the wrist will be lost and will also cause discomfort to the horse's mouth.

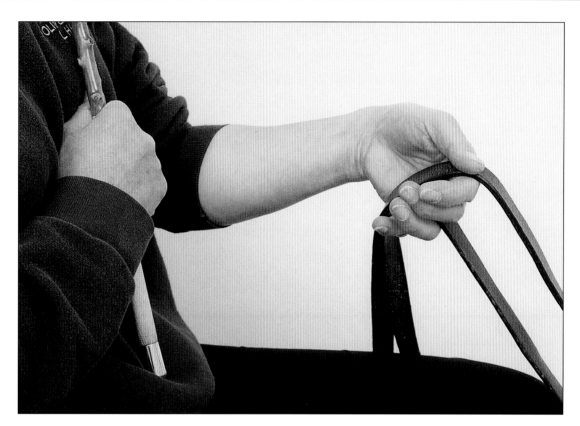

Collapsed wrist with open fingers (*above*) If this is allowed to happen the driver will have little or no control of the reins, and therefore little or no control of the horse!

Wrist dropped forward This will result in the horse continually veering to the right and necessitate the left rein being shortened.

Right hand flat on the reins If the right hand is placed flat on the top of the reins, instead of through the reins, the whip will be dropped into the horizontal position. This could cause the lash to become entangled in the wheel. It will also result in your passenger being continually hit with the whip.

'Cucumber sandwich syndrome' By picking up a rein between the index finger and the thumb of the right hand, the whip will drop forwards and hit the horse's hindquarters.

ACKNOWLEDGEMENTS

Our thanks to Dounhurst Mr. Mac, Nikki Haines and Rikke Neilson.

British Library Cataloguing-in-Publication Data.
A catalogue record for this book is available from the
British Library

ISBN 0.85131.726.X

Published in Great Britain in 1998 by
J. A. Allen & Company Limited,
1 Lower Grosvenor Place, Buckingham Palace Road,
London, SW1W OEL

Design and Typesetting by Paul Saunders
Series editor Jane Lake
Colour Separation by Tenon & Polert (H.K.) Ltd.
Printed in Hong Kong by Dah Hua Printing Press Co. Ltd.

'Plucking the cello' By pulling on the right rein in a backward and outward fashion the rein is pulled out of the left hand. When the right rein is released the horse will veer off to the left as the rein will have been lengthened.

AUTHOR'S NOTE ON GLOVES

It is strongly recommended that gloves are worn when driving. They should be brown leather and half a size too large; the loose fitting will allow for freedom of movement of the driver's fingers and help to prevent them becoming unnecessarily tired.

The author is not shown wearing gloves when demonstrating techniques on the driving apparatus thus ensuring that the position of her fingers and hands can be seen clearly.